Tommy Dee

Three Stars Still Shining

The story behind the first tribute song to Buddy Holly, The Big Bopper, and Ritchie Valens

Albert Leichter

Copyright © 2011 Albert Leichter

All Rights Reserved

No part of this book may be reproduced or transmitted in any form or by any means, electronic or mechanical, including photocopying, recording, or by any information storage and retrieval system without written permission from the publisher.

Part of a Sound Company founded in 1973

203 Skyland Drive, Suite C
Staunton, VA 24401-2358 USA
www.clocktowerpublications.com
trgww@ntelos.net

First Edition

ISBN 978-0-9704280-9-7

Acknowledgements

Thomas Donaldson

This work is based on an interview conducted with Thomas (Tommy Dee) Donaldson. He gave generously of his time and answered numerous questions about his career in the music business as radio announcer, singer, writer, record producer, television show host, and talent scout.

Dusty Donaldson

Dusty Donaldson, daughter of Thomas Donaldson, answered many questions and supplied invaluable information, pictures of her father, and many of the record labels reproduced here. Without her help, this work would not be possible. All photos and graphics used, unless otherwise noted, come from the Donaldson family files.

Cynthia Hughes

Cynthia Hughes, daughter of Thomas Donaldson, provided valuable information to help fill in some of the gaps in my research and was especially helpful in clarifying her father's movements around the country.

Kimberly Lester

Kimberly Lester, granddaughter of Thomas Donaldson, was kind enough to read the manuscript and offered many good suggestions for improving the readability of this work.

Charles Brand, Bruce Chase, Carolyn Shuey, and Harry Yeatts

I am also indebted to these close friends who made important suggestions to improve the manuscript.

Helene Leichter

My wife Helene has read every book I've written and always makes excellent suggestions. I am very grateful for her continued support.

Thomas "Tommy Dee" Donaldson c.1959

Preface

When Buddy Holly, the Big Bopper, and Ritchie Valens died in a plane crash on February 3, 1959, news of the tragedy spread quickly. The artists' families, the other artists on tour and the thousands of people who had seen them perform a few days or only hours before the accident were stunned.

Many people in the music business, including disc jockey Tommy Dee, could not believe it at first. Dee read the news on his radio station's Teletype and was traumatized. Recognizing instinctively that something significant had occurred, following his shift he wrote down his thoughts.

The artists' careers were just beginning but already well known to Dee and to rock and roll fans. Since the crash, interest in and demand for recordings and memorabilia by Holly, the Bopper, and Valens have steadily increased. Holly, in particular, has become one of the most influential and collected rock and roll artists of all time.

Although there would soon be other songs, Dee's *Three Stars* was the most successful tribute for a dozen years. I was familiar with the song and finally got to meet Tommy Dee in 1993. At that time he told me that he had not been interviewed since 1959 and his story had never been published. His story based on that interview was published in 1994. Since then, so much more information has become available that it was worth another look. This expanded work is the result of that research.

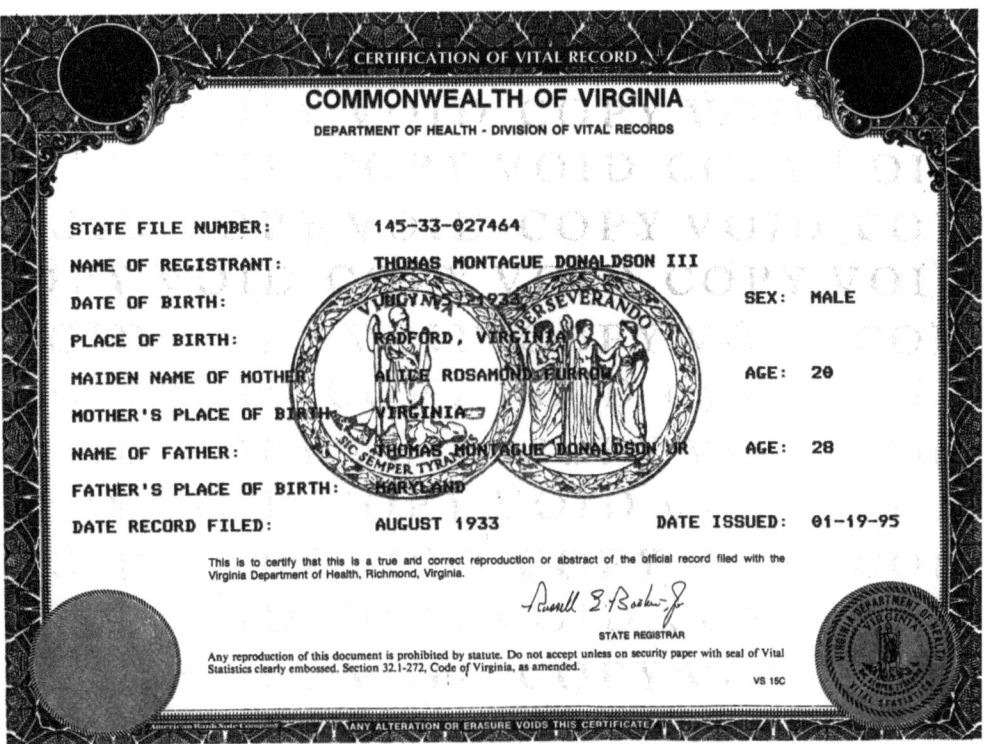

Birth certificate of Thomas Montague Donaldson, III

Thomas Montague Donaldson III, known professionally as Tommy Dee, was born on July 15, 1933, in Vicker, Virginia, located in southwest Virginia near Christiansburg. Not much is known about his childhood, but he served in the Marine Corps in the early 1950s. He married Helen Louise Bradley February 23, 1951. His first known radio job began in April 1958 as an announcer at KCLS in Flagstaff, Arizona. His next move was to KOFA in Yuma, where he worked from May 1958 to January 1959. He learned early in his career that being an announcer or disc jockey meant frequent moves from station to station, town to town, and often state to state. He was in his first week at KFXM in San Bernardino, California when the first tragedy of rock and roll occurred.

When Dee started at KFXM, the recording career of Buddy Holly (Charles Hardin Holley) was two years old, with one record (*Peggy Sue*) in the top 20 under his own name and three records under the Crickets' name (*That'll Be The*

Day, Oh, Boy!, and Maybe Baby). The Big Bopper (Jiles Perry Richardson, Jr.) who was also a disc jockey had one top 20 hit (Chantilly Lace). Ritchie Valens (Richard Steven Valenzuela) also had just one top 20 hit (Donna).

Holly, the Bopper, and Valens were the headliners of General Artist Corporation's *Winter Dance Party*, a series of concerts scheduled to run from January 23 to February 15, 1959. The timing was unusual as most upper Midwest tours were planned for the spring, summer, or early fall instead of the dead of winter.

The other recognizable name on the tour was Dion and the Belmonts whose only top 20 hit thus far was *No One Knows*. Then there was the little-known Frankie Sardo whose records never made it into the Top 100, although he later had a more successful film career. Eddie Cochran (Raymond Edward Cochran) was originally slated to be on the same bill but could not participate due to the filming of the movie *Go, Johnny, Go!* (Valens had completed his part in the film prior to the tour's start.) As it turned out, Cochran died 14 months after the crash as a result of a taxi accident in the United Kingdom. Gene Vincent (Vincent Eugene Craddock), best known for *Be-Bop-A-Lula*, had also been in the taxi and was fortunate having only suffered a broken collarbone.

The Winter Dance Party Itinerary, January 23 to February 15, 1959

January 23 George Devine's Million Dollar Ballroom, Milwaukee, Wisconsin
January 24 Eagles Ballroom, Kenosha, Wisconsin
January 25 Kato Ballroom, Mankato, Minnesota
January 26 Fournier's Ballroom, Eau Claire, Wisconsin
January 27 Fiesta Ballroom, Montevideo, Minnesota
January 28 Promenade Ballroom, St. Paul, Minnesota
January 29 Capitol Theatre, Davenport, Iowa
January 30 Laramar Ballroom, Fort Dodge, Iowa
January 31 Duluth National Guard Armory, Duluth, Minnesota
February 1 Cinderella Ballroom, Appleton, Wisconsin (cancelled)
February 1 Riverside Ballroom, Green Bay, Wisconsin
February 2 Surf Ballroom, Clear Lake, Iowa
February 3 The Armory, Moorhead, Minnesota
February 4 Shore Acres Ballroom, Sioux City, Iowa
February 5 Val Air Ballroom, Des Moines, Iowa
February 6 Danceland Ballroom, Cedar Rapids, Iowa
February 7 Les Buzz Ballroom, Spring Valley, Illinois

February   8 Aragon Ballroom, Chicago, Illinois
February   9 Hippodrome Auditorium, Waterloo, Iowa
February 10 Melody Hill, Dubuque, Iowa
February 11 Memorial Auditorium, Louisville, Kentucky
February 12 Memorial Auditorium, Canton, Ohio
February 13 Stanbaugh Auditorium, Youngstown, Ohio
February 14 The Armory, Peoria, Illinois
February 15 Illinois State Armory, Springfield, Illinois

Map of Winter Dance Party Tour, January 23 to February 2, 1959

Below are authentic Winter Dance Party Posters.

January 24
Eagles Ballroom
Kenosha, WI

January 25
Kato Ballroom
Mankato, MN

January 25
Kato Ballroom
Mankato, MN

January 26
Fournier's Ballroom
Eau Claire, WI

January 27
Fiesta Ballroom
Montevideo, MN

January 28
Promenade Ballroom
St. Paul, MN

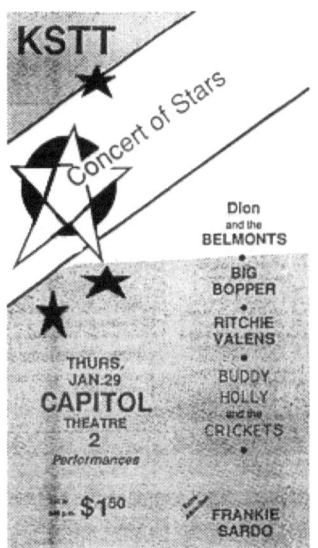

January 29
Capitol Theatre
Davenport, IA

January 30
Laramar Ballroom
Fort Dodge, IA

January 31
Duluth National Guard Armory
Duluth, MN

February 2
Surf Ballroom
Clear Lake, IA

2

The tour schedule would have been grueling enough had the buses been in top condition, but that was not the case. The buses broke down frequently and there were problems with the heaters, so that several vehicles were needed to get them through the schedule. In desperation over the transportation situation, the need to do laundry, and the desire to get some restful sleep, Holly chartered a plane for the Crickets. The Crickets at this time were composed of Tommy Allsup (lead guitar), Carl Bunch (drums), Waylon Jennings (bass), and himself, to fly to Fargo, North Dakota, the airport nearest to the next show at Moorhead, Minnesota. The Bopper felt ill and asked Jennings if he could have his seat on the plane and Jennings agreed. Valens challenged Allsup to a coin flip and won his place. Carl Bunch had temporarily dropped out of the tour while he was in the hospital being treated for frostbite due to riding in the unheated buses; either Holly or the Belmont's Carlo Mastrangelo had been filling in on drums in his absence.

Holly, the Bopper, and Valens arrived at the Mason City Municipal Airport at 12:40 a.m., February 3, 1959. According to the Civil Aeronautics Report, Roger Peterson, the pilot, had been checking the weather since 5:30 p.m. the previous day. Although he was told the weather was changing, he was not cautioned to postpone the flight. This was in line with Air Traffic Communications Station practices of leaving it to the pilot to request an interpretation of the facts supplied. The final report indicated that neither the pilot nor the airplane owner dug below the surface of the information supplied, that several weather advisories issued were not shared with either person, and the pilot's inexperience with instrument flying contributed to the accident. Peterson checked the weather again while he was taxiing to the end of the runway and made the decision to take off at 12:55 a.m., although there was light snow falling locally.

Immediately following takeoff, Peterson was to report his flight plan via radio but when he did not, airplane owner Hubert J. "Jerry" Dwyer became concerned and tried to contact the plane but was unsuccessful. By then, the weather had deteriorated to the point where Dwyer could not immediately begin an air search. Dwyer finally took off about 9:00 a.m. and at approximately 9:35 a.m. found the wreckage a few miles from the takeoff point in a cornfield covered with four inches of snow. The pilot and his three passengers were later confirmed to have been killed on impact.

3

Site of the airplane crash from the collection of Tommy Dee

The Civil Aeronautics Board Report

Aircraft Accident Report Adopted: September 15, 1959 Released: September 23, 1959 Mason City, Iowa

Synopsis

A Beech Bonanza, N3794N, crashed at night approximately 5 miles northwest of the Mason City Municipal Airport, Mason City, Iowa, at approximately 0100, February 3, 1959. The pilot and three passengers were killed and the aircraft was demolished.

The aircraft was observed to take off toward the south in a normal manner, turn and climb to an estimated altitude of 800 feet, and then head in a northwesterly direction. When approximately 5 miles had been traversed, the tail light of the aircraft was seen to descend gradually until it disappeared from sight. Following this, many unsuccessful attempts were made to contact the aircraft by radio. The wreckage was found in a [field] later that morning.

This accident, like so many before it, was caused by the pilot's decision to undertake a flight in which the likelihood of encountering instrument conditions existed, in the mistaken belief that he could cope with en route instrument weather conditions, without having the necessary familiarization with the instruments in the aircraft and without being properly certificated to fly solely by instruments.

Investigation

Charles Hardin [Holly], J.P. Richardson, and Richard Valenzuela were members of a group of entertainers appearing in Clear Lake, Iowa, the night of Feb. 2, 1959. The following night they were to appear in Moorhead, Minnesota. Because of bus trouble, which had plagued the group, these three decided to go to Moorhead ahead of the others. Accordingly, arrangements were made through Roger Peterson of the Dwyer Flying Service, Inc., located [at] the Mason City Airport, to charter an aircraft to fly to Fargo, North Dakota, the nearest airport to Moorhead.

At approximately 1730, Pilot Peterson went to the Air Traffic Communications Station (ATCS), which was located in a tower on top of the Administration Building, to obtain the necessary weather information pertinent to the flight. This included the current weather at Mason City, Iowa; Minneapolis, Redwood Falls, and Alexandria, Minnesota and the terminal forecast for Fargo, North Dakota. He was advised by the communicator that all these stations were reporting ceilings of 5,000 feet or better and visibility of 10 miles or above; also, that the Fargo terminal forecast indicated the possibility of light snow showers after 0200 and a cold frontal passage about 0400. The communicator told Peterson that a later terminal forecast would be available at 2300. At 2200 and again at 2330 Pilot Peterson called ATCS concerning the weather. At the latter time he was advised that the stations en route were reporting ceilings of 4200 feet or better with visibility still 10 miles or greater. Light snow was reported at Minneapolis. The cold front previously reported by the communicator as forecast to pass Fargo at 0400 was now reported to pass there at 0200. The Mason City weather was reported to the pilot as:

ceiling measured 6,000 overcast; visibility 15 miles plus; temperature 15 degrees; dew point 8 degrees; wind south 25 to 32 knots; altimeter setting 29.96 inches.

At 2355, Peterson, accompanied by Hubert Dwyer, a certificated commercial pilot, the local fixed-base operator at the Mason City Airport, and owner of Bonanza N3794N (the aircraft used on the flight), again went to ATCS for the latest weather information. The local weather had changed somewhat in that the ceiling had lowered to 5,000 feet, light snow was falling, and the altimeter setting was now 29.90 inches.

The passengers arrived at the airport about 0040 and after their baggage had been stowed on board, the pilot and passengers boarded the aircraft. Pilot Peterson told Mr. Dwyer that he would file his flight plan by radio when airborne. While the aircraft was being taxied to the end of runway 17, Peterson called ATCS and asked for the latest local and en route weather. This was given him as not having changed materially en route; however, the local weather was now reported as: precipitation ceiling 3,000 feet, sky obscured; visibility 6 miles; light snow; wind south 20 knots, gusts to 30 knots; altimeter setting 29.85 inches.

A normal takeoff was made at [0055] and the aircraft was observed to make a left 180-degree turn and climb to approximately 800 feet and then, after passing the airport to the east, to head in a northwesterly direction. Through most of the flight the tail light of the aircraft was plainly visible to Mr. Dwyer, who was watching from a platform outside the tower. When about five miles from the airport, Dwyer saw the tail light of the aircraft gradually descend until out of sight. When Peterson did not report his flight plan by radio soon after takeoff, the communicator, at Mr. Dwyer's request, repeatedly tried to reach him but was unable to do so. The time was approximately 0100.

After an extensive air search, the wreckage of N3794N was sighted in an open farm field at approximately 0935 that morning. All occupants were dead and the aircraft was demolished. The field in which the aircraft was found was level and covered with about four inches of snow.

The accident occurred in a sparsely inhabited area and there were [no] witnesses. Examination of the wreckage indicated that the first impact with the ground was made by the right wing tip when the aircraft was in a steep right bank and in a nose-low attitude. It was further determined that the aircraft was traveling at high speed on a heading of 315 degrees. Parts were scattered over a distance of 540 feet, at the end of which the main wreckage was found lying against a barbed wire fence. The three passengers were thrown clear of the wreckage, the pilot was found in the cockpit. The two front seat safety belts and the middle ones of the rear seat were torn free [from] their attach points. The two rear outside belt ends remained attached to their respective fittings; the buckle of one was broken. None of the webbing was broken and no belts were about the occupants.

Although the aircraft was badly damaged, certain important facts were determined. There was no fire. All components were accounted [for] at the wreckage site. There was no evidence of inflight structural failure or failure of the controls. The landing gear was retracted at the time of impact. The damaged engine was dismantled and examined; there was no evidence of engine malfunctioning or failure in flight. Both blades of the propeller were broken at the hub, giving evidence that the engine was producing power when ground impact occurred. The hub pitch-change mechanisms indicated that the blade pitch was in the cruise range.

Despite the damage to the cockpit the following readings were obtained:
Magneto switches were both in the "off" position.
Battery and generator switches were in the "on" position.
The tachometer r.p.m. needle was stuck at 2200.
Fuel pressure, oil temperature and pressure gauges were stuck in the normal or green range.
The attitude gyro indicator was stuck in a manner indicative of a 90-degree angle.
The rate of climb indicator was stuck at 3,000-feet-per-minute descent.
The airspeed indicator needle was stuck between 165-170 mph.
The directional gyro was caged.
The omni selector was positioned at 114.9, the frequency of the Mason City omni range.
The course selector indicated a 360-degree course.
The transmitter was tuned to 122.1, the frequency for Mason City.
The Lear autopilot was not operable.

The Aircraft

The aircraft, a Beech Bonanza, model 35, S/N-1019, identification N3794N, was manufactured October 17, 1947. It was powered by a Continental model E185-8 engine which had a total of 40 hours since major overhaul. The aircraft was purchased by the Dwyer Flying Service, July 1, 1958, and, according to records and the testimony of the licensed mechanic employed by Dwyer, had been properly maintained since its acquisition. N3794N was equipped with high and low frequency radio transmitters and receivers, a Narca omnigator, Lear autopilot (only recently installed and not operable), all the necessary engine and navigational instruments, and a full panel of instruments used for instrument flying, including a Sperry F3 attitude Gyro.

Pilot

Roger Arthur Peters[on], 21 years old, was regularly employed by Dwyer Flying Service as a commercial pilot and flight instructor, and had been with them [a]bout one year. He had been flying since October of 1954, and had accumulated 711 flying hours, of which 128 were in Bonanza aircraft. Almost all of the Bonanza time was acquired during charter flights. He had approximately 52 hours of dual instrument training and had passed his instrument written examination. He fail[ed] an instrument flight check on March 21, 1958, [10] months prior to the accident. His last CAA second-class physical examination was taken March 29, 1958. A hearing deficiency of his right ear was found and because of this he was given a flight test. A waiver noting this hearing deficiency was issued November 29, 1958. According to his associates, he was a young married man who built his life around flying. When his instrument training was taken, several aircraft were used and these were all equipped with the conventional type artificial horizon and none with the Sperry Attitude Gyro such as was installed in Bonanza N3794N. These two instruments differ greatly in their pictorial display.

The conventional artificial horizon provides a direct reading indication of the bank and pitch attitude of the aircraft which is accurately indicated by a miniature aircraft pictorially displayed against a horizon bar and as if observed from the rear. The Sperry F3 gyro also provides a direct reading indication of the bank and pitch attitude of the aircraft, but its pictorial presentation is achieved by using a stabilized sphere whose free-floating movements behind a miniature aircraft presents pitch information with a sensing exactly opposite from that depicted by the conventional artificial horizon.

The Weather

The surface weather chart for 0000 February 3, 1959, showed a cold front extending from [t]he northwestern corner of Minnesota through central Nebraska with a secondary cold front through North Dakota. Widespread snow shower activity was indicated in advance of these fronts. Temperatures along the airway route [from] Mason City to Fargo were below freezing at all levels with an inversion between 3,000 and 4,000 feet and abundant moisture present at all levels through 12,000 feet. The temperature and moisture content was such that moderate to heavy icing and precipitation existed in the clouds along the route. Winds aloft along the route at altitudes below 10,000 feet were reported to be 30 to 50 knots from [the] southwesterly direction, with [t]he strongest winds indicated to be closest to the cold front.

A flash advisory issued by the U.S. Weather Bureau at Minneapolis at 2335 on February 2 contained the following information: Flash Advisory No. 5 A band of snow about 100 miles wide at 2335 from extreme northwestern Minnesota, northern North Dakota through Bismarck and south-southwestward through [the] Black Hills of South Dakota with visibility generally below 2 miles in snow. This area or band moving southeastward about 25 knots, cold front at 2335 from vicinity Winnipeg through Minot, Williston, moving southeastward 25 to 30 knots with surface winds following front north-northwest with 25 to gusts of 45. Valid until 0335.

Another advisory issued by the U. S. Weather Bureau at Kansas City, Missouri at 0015 on February 3 was: Flash Advisory No. 1. Over [the] eastern half of Kansas ceilings are locally below one thousand feet, visibilities locally 2 miles or less in freezing drizzle, light snow and fog. Moderate to locally heavy icing areas of freezing drizzle and locally moderate icing in clouds below 10,000 feet over eastern portion Nebraska, Kansas, northwest Missouri and most of Iowa. Valid until 0515. Neither communicator could recall having drawn these flash advisories to the attention of Pilot Peterson. Mr. Dwyer said that when he accompanied pilot Peterson to ATCS, no information was given them indicating instrument flying weather would be encountered along the route.

Analysis

There is no evidence to indicate that very important flash advisories regarding adverse weather conditions were drawn to the attention of the pilot. On the contrary, there is evidence that the weather briefing consisted solely of the reading of current weather at en route terminal and terminal forecasts for the destination. Failure of the communicators to draw these advisories to the attention of the pilot and to emphasize their importance could readily lead the pilot to underestimate the severity of the weather situation.

It must be pointed out that the communicators' responsibility with respect to furnishing weather information to pilots is to give them all the available information, to interpret this data if requested, but not to advise in any manner. Also, the pilot and the operator in this case had a definite responsibility to request and obtain all of the available information and to interpret it correctly.

Mr. Dwyer said that he had confidence in Peterson and relied entirely on his operational judgment with respect to the planning and conduct of the flight.

At Mason City, at the time of takeoff, the barometer was falling, the ceiling and visibility were lowering, light snow had begun to fall, and the surface winds and winds aloft were so high one could reasonably have expected to encounter adverse weather during the estimated two-hour flight.

It was already snowing at Minneapolis, and the general forecast for the area along the intended route indicated deteriorating weather conditions. Considering all of these facts and the fact that the company was certificated to fly in accordance with visual flight rules only, both day and night, together with the pilot's unproved ability to fly by instrument, the decision to go seems most imprudent.

It is believe[d] that shortly after takeoff pilot Peterson entered an area of complete darkness and one in which there was no definite horizon; that the snow conditions and the lack of horizon required him to rely solely on flight instruments for aircraft attitude and orientation.

The high gusty winds and the attendant turbulence which existed this night would have caused the rate of climb indicator and the turn and bank indicator to fluctuate to such an extent that an interpretation of these instruments so far as attitude control is concerned would have been difficult to a pilot as inexperienced as Peterson. The airspeed and altimeter alone would not have provided him with sufficient reference to maintain control of the pitch attitude. With his limited experience the pilot would tend to rely on the attitude gyro which is relatively stable under these conditions.

Service experience with the use of the attitude gyro has clearly indicated confusion among pilots during the transition period or when alternating between conventional and attitude gyros. Since Peterson had received his instrument training in aircraft equipped with the conventional type artificial horizon, and since this instrument and the attitude gyro are opposite in their pictorial display of the pitch attitude, it is probabl[e] that the reverse sensing would at times produce reverse control action. This is especially true of instrument flight conditions requiring a high degree of concentration or requiring multiple function, as would be the case when flying instrument conditions in turbulence without a copilot. The directional gyro was found caged and it is possible that it was never used during the short flight. However, this evidence is not conclusive. If the directional gyro [was] caged throughout the flight this could only have added to the pilot's confusion.

Conclusion

At night, with an overcast sky, snow falling, no definite horizon, and a proposed flight over a sparsely settled area with an absence of ground lights, a requirement for control of the aircraft solely by reference to flight instruments can be predicated with virtual certainty.

The Board concludes that pilot Peterson, when a short distance from the airport, was confronted with this situation. Because of fluctuation of the rate instruments caused by gusty winds he would have been forced to concentrate and rely greatly on the attitude gyro, an instrument with which he was not completely familiar. The pitch display of this instrument is the reverse of the instrument he was accustomed to; therefore, he could have become confused and thought that he was making a climbing turn when in reality he was making a descending turn. The fact that the aircraft struck the ground in a steep turn but with the nose lowered only slightly, indicates that some control was being affected at the time. The weather briefing supplied to the pilot was seriously inadequate in that it failed to even mention adverse flying conditions which should have been highlighted.

Probable Cause

The Board determines that [the] [probable] cause of this accident was the pilot's unwise decision to embark on a flight which would necessitate flying solely by instruments when he was not properly certificated or qualified to do so. Contributing factors were serious deficiencies in the weather briefing, and the pilot's unfamiliarity with the instrument which determines the attitude of the aircraft.

By the Civil Aeronautics Board: James R. Dupree/Chan Gurney/ Harmar D. Denny/G. Joseph Minetti/Louis J. Hector

4

The other artists traveling by bus didn't realize what had happened until they arrived at Moorhead City. As it turned out, the bus trip from Clear Lake to Moorhead City would be one of the easiest of the entire tour.

Following news of the crash, General Artist Corporation initially canceled the tour. Rod Lucier, a disc jockey at KVOX in Moorhead City and promoter of the February 3 show, began getting the word out about the cancellation. However, the public response was very supportive for going on with the show, and after speaking with the remaining artists the concert continued as scheduled.

Bobby Vee (Robert Thomas Velline) who was still in high school and knew Holly's songs filled in with his band, the Shadows, on February 3. At this time, Vee was unknown beyond the local area and still unrecorded.

General Artist Corporation supplied two new headliners, Frankie Avalon and Jimmy Clanton (who also appeared in *Go, Johnny, Go*). Avalon left three days prior to the end of the tour and his slot was filled by Fabian (Forte). Debbie Stevens, the wife of disc jockey Jim Lounsbury and promoter of the January 24 show was also added. She had recorded (but had no hits) under a variety of names in the late 1950s. As Debbie Dean, she was the first white artist signed to the Motown record label and recorded *Don't Let Him Shop Around*, Billboard number 92, an answer to the Miracles' *Shop Around*. Ronnie Smith, who had previously recorded with Tommy Allsup and Carl Bunch as Ronnie Smith and the Poor Boys, was brought in to take over as lead vocalist of the Crickets for the remainder of the tour. Dion and the Belmonts and Frankie Sardo completed the tour as contracted.

5

"I wrote that song," Tommy Dee said speaking of *Three Stars*, "right after they died. I was on the air at KFXM in San Bernardino. The bells went crazy on the Teletype. 'What is this?' I started reading it, then poured my heart out. 'No, it can't be true.' So as soon as I got off, I wrote *Three Stars* in about 20 minutes. My friend next door had a little Webcor [tape recorder]. I just put it down as I wrote it, with just a strum of the guitar. He said 'You could do a record on that.' I said I would just play it on my show. All I meant for it to be was a tribute.

"A writer never knows," Dee continued. "I talk frequently with Bobby Helms, who's a good friend of mine. He did *Fraulein* and *Jingle Bell Rock*, but he hated both of them. He didn't want to cut them. They set up three different sessions for *Jingle Bell Rock* and he didn't make any of them. Finally they said, 'Bobby you get down here Friday and record *Jingle Bell Rock* or you're off the label.' But the reason he didn't like it was because of the person who recorded the demo." As it turned out, Helms' recording of *Jingle Bell Rock* hit the charts in 1957, 1958, 1960, 1961, and 1962, and can still be heard on the radio each Christmas.

Dee soon had a change of heart about having *Three Stars* recorded. "I went over to American Music [on Thursday, February 5] and played it for one of their people. He listened to the song, went out and brought in someone I didn't know. After he listened to it they played it again. They went out into the hall and whispered. I was wondering if they were trying to steal my song. They came back in and the first guy said 'This is Sylvester Cross who owns American Music.' Cross said, 'Do you mind if Eddie Cochran cuts this song?' I said, 'No.'

"Jerry Capehart, who produced Cochran's songs, lived about two blocks away. They called him and he came right down with Cochran, who happened to be in his apartment." Cochran had previously recorded for Cross' Crest Records, but was now signed to the Liberty label. They listened to Dee's original tape. Dee continued, "Eddie, in tears, said, 'Let's cut it right now.' They went right over to the Liberty studios. He was in there about two or three hours, with his guitar. It just didn't come off."

Three Stars (as recorded by Eddie Cochran)

1,2,3 (probably shouted out by Jerry Capehart)
Look up in the sky, up towards the north.
There are three new stars, brightly shining forth.
They're shining oh-so bright from heaven above.
Gee, we're gonna miss you, everybody sends their love.

Ritchie, you were just starting to realize your dreams.
Everyone calls me a kid, but you were only seventeen.
Now Almighty God has called you, oh-so far away.
Maybe it's to save some boy or girl, who might have gone astray.
And with your star shining through the dark and lonely night.
To light the path and show the way, the way that's right.
Gee, we're gonna miss you, everybody sends their love.

Buddy, I can still see you, with that shy grin on your face.
Seems like your hair was always a little messed up, and kinda outa place.
Now, not many people actually knew you or understood how you felt.
But just a song from, just a song from you could make the coldest heart melt.
Well you're singing for God now, in His chorus in the sky.
Buddy Holly, I'll always remember you with tears in my eyes.
Gee, we're gonna miss you, everybody sends their love.

I see a stout man, the Big Bopper's your name.
God called you to heaven, maybe for, for new fortune and fame.
Keep wearing that big Stetson hat and ramble up to the mic.
And don't forget those wonderful words, 'You know what I like.'

Look up in the sky, up towards the north.
There are three new stars, brightly shining forth.
They're shining oh-so bright from heaven above.
Gee, we're gonna miss you, everybody sends their love.

THREE STARS
Words and Music by THOMAS DONALDSON
© 1959 (Renewed) UNICHAPPELL MUSIC INC. (BMI) and ELVIS PRESLEY MUSIC, INC. (BMI)
All Rights Administered by UNICHAPPELL MUSIC INC.
All Rights Reserved   Used by Permission

Eddie Cochran's recording of *Three Stars* was not released at the time but came out as a single 45 RPM in the United Kingdom in 1966, and in the United States in 1971 on a United Artists (which by then owned the Liberty catalog) double album simply titled *Eddie Cochran*. The liner notes on the album state "*Three Stars* was originally designed as a record to garner royalties for the three stars' families; but there was some problem in the details of this agreement with Liberty [Records] and it was never released."

Dee disputed the idea that such a project was ever mentioned at the time. Rather, he said, "The record was just a bad recording. He was trying to talk through the record. He was so broke up by it; he and Buddy Holly were very close friends."

Once it was decided that Cochran's recording would not be issued, American Music sought out Paul Anka, George Hamilton IV, and Johnny Nash to record the song together as they had done with the 1958 top 30 hit *The Teen Commandments*, but Anka was in Europe and couldn't get back.

6

First Pressing

"I never believed that the thing would be a hit and I never thought of recording it myself," Dee insisted. "It was the furthest thing from my mind." But on Monday, February 9, Dee was told that Liberty would not issue Cochran's version, and American Music had decided to cut it with him. Dee went down to Gold Star Studios in Hollywood where he recorded the song at 9:00 p.m. Gold Star was a state-of-the-art studio with a great echo chamber. The song was recorded on a two-track machine so that it was available in that format (for the new stereo jukeboxes) as well as in monoraul. Gold Star was also the studio where Ritchie Valens recorded *Come on Let's Go*, *Donna*, and *La Bamba*. Gold Star later became famous as the studio where Phil Spector created his "Wall of Sound" recordings.

"They wanted a female voice [on the record]," Dee said. "Carol Kay, an act that American Music was already working with was chosen. She got paid $50.00 for the part. She was a very important part of that record. She did a wonderful job. There would not have been a record without her."

Tommy, Carol, and the Teen-Aires only got to practice *Three Stars* one time with the band, because studio time was a luxury and session musicians had to be paid scale. Tommy spoke the recitation while Carol and the group provided the chorus. The "B" side of the record was called *I'll Never Change* and just featured Carol Kay and the Teen-Aires.

Three Stars (as recorded by Tommy Dee, Carol Kay, and the Teen-Aires)

Look up in the sky, up towards the north.
There are three new stars, brightly shining forth.
They're shining so bright, from heaven above.
Gee we're gonna miss you, everybody sends their love.

On the left stands Ritchie Valens, a young boy just seventeen.
Just beginning to realize and explore, his teenage dreams.
Why did God call him oh so far away.
Maybe to help some boy or girl who might have gone astray.
With his star shining in the dark, a lonely night to light the path.
And, show the way, the way that's right.
Gee we're gonna miss you, everybody sends their love.

On the right stands Buddy Holly, with a shy grin on his face.
Funny how you always seem to notice, that one little curl out of place.
Not many people really knew Buddy, or understood how he felt.
But just a song from his lips, would make the coldest heart melt.
Buddy's singing for God now, His chorus in the sky.
Buddy Holly, we'll always remember you with tears in our eyes.
Gee we're gonna miss you, everybody sends their love.

In the middle stands a stout man, the Big Bopper is his name.
Now God has called him, perhaps to new fortune and fame.
He wore a big Stetson hat, and sort of rambled up to the mic.
How can we ever forget those wonderful words, 'You know what I like.'

Look up in the sky, up towards the north.
There are three new stars, brightly shining forth.
They're shining so bright from heaven above.
Gee we're gonna miss you, everybody sends their love.

THREE STARS
Words and Music by THOMAS DONALDSON
© 1959 (Renewed) UNICHAPPELL MUSIC INC. (BMI) and ELVIS PRESLEY MUSIC, INC. (BMI)
All Rights Administered by UNICHAPPELL MUSIC INC.
All Rights Reserved   Used by Permission

Tommy said, "I took the acetate [a record made directly from the original master tape] back to the radio station. I gave it to the all night man. I said, 'Here's my new record. Give it a play, if you get a chance.' I didn't have a radio in my car. I had a '47 Mercury; the radio was out. I couldn't even listen to it.

"When I came in the next day, I had messages from all these record stores. 'Boy, look at all these calls for you,'" the radio station staff told him. "I called the record stores. They said, 'Is that your record?' I said, 'Yes.' They said, 'I want 1,500; I want 1,000; 2,500.' So I called Sylvester Cross. I told the man. I can still hear him say, 'Now Tommy, don't try to con me.' I said, 'Well, call these people.'

"A couple of hours later he called me. He said, 'We'll have records on Wednesday. Come down and get them.' So I sold the first 12,000." The record was released on American Music's Crest Records subsidiary (distributed by Starday Records) on Wednesday, February 11, eight days after the crash.

"I'll tell you," Tommy continued, "what really influenced me in my writing. It was just an old Luke the Drifter [Hank Williams] kind of thing. When I started to write it, I didn't realize it but it was like his recitations. That's just a basic country format.

"Back in the old days," Dee continued, "when you listened to the radio you had to search [the dial] far and away. I would try to tune in late at night. I was the only one in my family who was into music, but I always liked it. Radio formats were not like today. It used to be across the South that you'd open up in the morning with country music, then you'd have a block of black programming, rhythm and blues, and then from 2 to 6 or until sign off you'd have country again. I just left the radio on all day so I listened to country and black music.

"I could never believe that the record would keep selling like that. When I'd go out [on tour] the audience would just cry. The best part about that record is when I was driving anywhere in the country I could hear the record being played [on the radio]. That's really a nice feeling.

"My record," Dee admitted, "was in the true sense of the word, a novelty record. I was in the right place at the right time. Everything just fell into place." Tommy didn't consider himself a great singer, but he did know how to work the crowd. "I had enough radio smarts in me to make it work."

Three Stars wasn't an immediate hit though. The record took almost two months to get onto the *Billboard Hot 100* chart, first appearing on April 5, 1959.

But once it started climbing, it reached number 11 and was on the charts for a total of 12 weeks. In the other leading weekly music magazine, *Cash Box*, the song reached number 16 and remained on the charts for six weeks. These are impressive figures considering the record was released on a small label the size of Crest Records.

Crest Records had a varied catalogue that included pop, rhythm and blues, country, rock-a-billy, and gospel. Their only national hits were *Three Stars* and *You're the Reason* by Bobby Edwards and the Four Young Men (*Billboard* number 11 in 1961). Glen Campbell had a minor hit on Crest with *Turn Around, Look at Me* (*Billboard* number 62 in 1961). In the early 1960s, Campbell was better known as a session musician or as a member of the instrumental group the Champs, following their hit *Tequila*. It wasn't until 1967 that Campbell's string of hits began at Capitol Records.

Three Stars was popular enough to warrant being issued outside the United States including Australia, Canada, and the United Kingdom. A sampling of how the song scored on radio stations in the spring of 1959 is shown below.

KATR, Corpus Christie, Texas, #7, April 18
KKWK, St. Louis, Missouri, #11, April 19
WKBW, Buffalo, New York, #12, April 24
KNUZ, Houston, Texas, #18, April 24
WKBR, Manchester, New Hampshire, #14, May 12
CHUM, Toronto, Canada, #32, May 25
KIOA, Des Moines, Iowa, #2, April 18

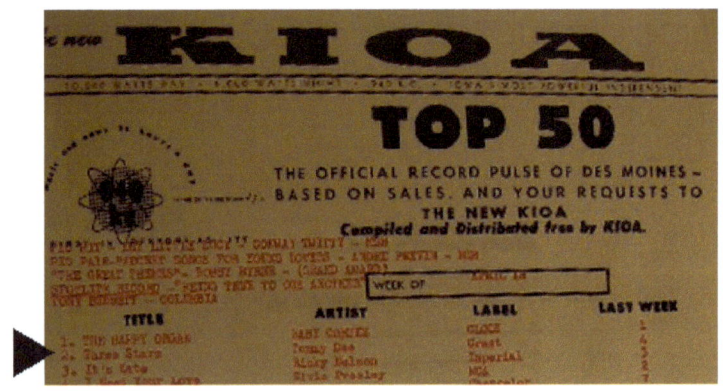

An early 1959 pressing of *Three Stars* on the Australian Columbia Records label
(Courtesy of Vinyl Solutions, Victoria, Australia)

A late 1959 or early 1960 pressing of *Three Stars* and *I'll Never Change* on the Australian Columbia Records shows that there were enough sales to warrant a second issuance of the song
(Courtesy of Plastic Passion, Western Australia, Australia)

Three Stars and *I'll Never Change* on Canada's Reo Records

7

Ruby Wright's *Three Stars* on King Records (courtesy of Andreas Hemmingsson)

Ruby Wright's *Three Stars* on United Kingdom's Parlophone label with original sleeve

As Dee's recording was hitting the national charts, King Records issued a version by Ruby Wright. Despite being well connected as the daughter of Kitty Wells and Johnny Wright, she had been recording for King since 1949 and never had a national hit. Ruby's *Three Stars* made it to only number 99 on the pop charts in the United States. However, her disc did better in the United Kingdom where Holly was very popular and King Records had a better distribution system than Crest Records. Wright's version (with Dick Pike, a disc jockey at WNOP in Newport, Kentucky, doing the recitation) hit number 19 in the United Kingdom.

Dee remembered, "At that time you couldn't get my record anywhere. They almost had to go to Mexico to press records, because we couldn't find enough [pressing] plants here. It was so bad that everybody; staff writers and everybody who worked for American Music had to go in to press the record. Even Eddie Cochran and Jerry Capehart came in and helped. Eddie was proud of the song. He loved it."

Many singers of the 1950s were never adequately paid for their efforts. Holly, the Bopper, Valens, and their families, for example, never believed they were sufficiently compensated for sales of their recordings. In contrast, Dee said,

"Crest treated me very well, better than a major label. When I first started the contract called for a penny a record. They tore that up and went to two cents a record. Then they tore that up and it finally went to four cents a record, and I was only on one side! I thought that was pretty good. I [eventually] got paid on four and a half million records."

Second Pressing

One long-standing mystery regarding *Three Stars* was cleared up by Dee. The record came out with two different group names: the first version listed Carol Kay and the Teen-Aires, while the second pressing showed the Teen Tones with no mention of Carol Kay on either side. Tommy remembered, "They [American Music] were afraid the Teen-Aires [name] was close to another group and they would get it confused. So they switched. I remember there was a discussion then, but I didn't pay much attention to it. So I really wasn't worried about the [two different] names. I remember they were afraid and they were saying that they might sue us. So Sylvester Cross said, 'If they're going to sue us let's change it.'"

To support record sales Dee would occasionally go out on the road but he didn't have a regular band. "I worked with Gene Vincent's Blue Caps [based in Norfolk, Virginia] quite a bit. I also worked with a group called the Big Beats out of Minneapolis. I went out with Eddie Cochran and Conway Twitty. We'd just go in and do the song and get off the stage. Sometimes I carried a guy named Bobby Lance.

"The next release I had was called *The Chair*, backed with *Hello, Lonesome*, also in 1959." This recording again featured the backup of Carol Kay and the Teen-Aires. Tommy remembered being scheduled to record *Deck of Cards*, but for a reason unknown to him it didn't happen. Instead, Wink Martindale, also a disc jockey, had a hit with it in 1959, as had T. Texas Tyler, Tex Ritter, and Phil Harris in the 1940s. Tyler is considered to have been the writer, but the idea goes back to at least the 18 century and may even be older.

After two months at KFXM, Dee moved to San Fernando and took an announcing job at KTYM, a country music station, in Inglewood, California.

Dee's last recording for Crest, also in 1959, was *Merry Christmas, Mary*. When asked about the song, he said, "It's best to be forgotten. It was just a Christmas record but it just didn't come off. I just wasn't happy with it. We were in a hurry to get it out [in time to sell for the Christmas Season]. It was a good song but it was just one of those things that didn't gel right. Matter of fact, the other side, *Angel of Love* was better."

In 1960 Dee left Crest Records and began recording for the Challenge label owned by Gene Autry and several partners. "I next did *There's A Star Spangled Banner Waving Somewhere*." The song had been a popular World War II number for Elton Britt (number 7, 1942) and Jimmy Wakely (number 14, 1943). Dee recorded the song in a patriotic fervor when Gary Francis Powers, who was piloting a CIA U-2 spy plane, was shot down over the Soviet Union. The other side was *Hobo and the Puppy*. His second and last release for Challenge, also in 1960, was *Ballad of a Drag Race,* backed with *The Story of Susie*.

From October 1960 to August 1964, Dee worked at KUZZ in Bakersfield, California. In 1963, Dee and his wife Helen purchased a ranch and built a recording studio in a separate building on its grounds. In 1963, one of their nine children died in an accident on the ranch. When Dee later established his publishing arm he named it Little Bill Music in his son's honor. In 1961 Dee recorded *A Little Dog Cried* and *Look Homeward Dear Angel*, issued on the Pike label. In 1963, Dee re-released *Look Homeward Dear Angel* backed with *Missing on a Mountain,* a tribute to Patsy Cline, Hawkshaw Hawkins, and Cowboy Copas, who died March 5, 1963 in an airplane accident. Despite the obvious potential of the "B" side of the record, it didn't do well. This record was also issued as *Look Homeward Dead Angel*.

Tommy Dee maintained his job as an announcer or disc jockey the entire time he was recording. "When I cut *Three Stars*, I was working rock. Then I went to Bakersfield (KUZZ radio station) where I also had a TV show. Met Merle Haggard and Bonnie Owens. We had a live show every day from 9:00 p.m. to 10:00 p.m. I cut the first thing Merle ever did. I had a handshake deal to record Merle but then lost him. We had him do two songs a week on the show. They were always Lefty Frizzell songs. That's where he really developed his style. He really had the potential to be a great artist. I remember a time when we used to pay Buck Owens $8 a night on the show. I remember when he couldn't even pay his phone bill. He was a great guitar picker."

At the end of 1963, Dee came out with *Open Letter*, a tribute to President Kennedy. "That record started off like a house on fire. I gave it to a distributing company in Los Angeles and then it died. I lost it." Dee believed that the record could have been a much bigger seller had the company pushed sales. "But," Dee continued, "We did over 100,000 overnight. I was afraid I was going to lose it [and] that's why I went to the distributor. The other side of that was *She Called Me Baby, Baby All Night Long*."

In August of 1964, Dee left Bakersfield and moved back to Virginia, where he operated the Top Hat Restaurant in Newport News until June of 1966. He then left the state and began work at WNFO-FM, the number three station behind WSM-FM and WLAC-FM in the Nashville, Tennessee market. In 1966 he also recorded two records for the Sims label, *Missing While Surfing* backed with *Goodbye High School* and *How's Your Momma 'Em* with the previously released *Goodbye High School*.

Dee's next move was back to Virginia where he joined WTID-FM, a 24-hour stereo station in Newport News, which first came on the air in the summer of 1967. But his stay in Virginia didn't last long. Dee said, "I had gotten out of music. I had a good job. I was making big money, but I wasn't happy. Then all these songs just started pouring out of me, 50 songs in 20 days. I said, 'We gotta go back to Nashville. So we moved back and I started working on Johnny Paycheck's label, Little Darlin' Records [Aubrey Mayhew was co-owner]. I started running their publishing company and working the studio. I was lucky enough to get right back in. I worked with them awhile [Little Darlin' Records was in business from 1966 to 1969] and I've been out on my own ever since. I've had over a hundred songs that I've written on the charts, but they weren't all big records."

In 1967, Dee recorded *School for Boys,* backed with *Roger, Ed and Gus (America's Astronaut Heroes)* for Starday Records. The latter title was a tribute to Apollo 1 astronauts Roger Chaffee, Edward White, and Virgil "Gus" Grissom who died January 27, 1967 when their command module caught fire on the launch pad.

About 1968 Dee joined WMTS radio station in Murfreesboro, Tennessee. Shortly thereafter, he bought radio station WJOE in Port St. Joe, Florida where he also served as general manager and announcer. He cut a cover of Guy Drake's *Welfare Cadillac,* most likely at WJOE's studios. The other side was *Puppy and the Hobo,* which was especially popular in Australia where it sold about 50,000 records. They tried to book him for a tour but Dee didn't fly which may have been due to the crash that took the lives of Holly, the Bopper, and Valens, and was the impetus for *Three Stars*.

In 1976, Dee returned to Virginia where he worked at WZAM in Norfolk. Never a person to do just one thing at a time, stay in one job or even in one location very long, in addition to playing records on the air he also performed at various clubs in the Tidewater area.

Business cards from the late 1970s

Tommy Dee at WZAM, Norfolk, Virginia, c. 1977/78

Tommy Dee at WZAM, Norfolk, Virginia, c. 1977/78

It took more than placing records on turntables to be a disc jockey; it took a bit of theatrics as well. Above, Tommy Dee is first "choked" then makes up with a "gorilla," at WZAM, Norfolk, Virginia, c. 1977/78

Signs advertising Tommy Dee appearances, late 1970s

Tommy Dee performing in these undated photographs

8

Tommy summed up his philosophy: "I'm not in the music business to make a lot of money. I'm in it to create something. It's like painting a picture. I enjoy helping young people get into the business. I don't have any investors to pay back. If he hits... Like they say, you roll the dice and take a chance."

Despite his extensive career as radio announcer, singer, writer, record producer, television show host, and talent scout, Dee never forgot *Three Stars*. As stock of his biggest hit would run low, he would press more records. Other record labels not associated with Dee such as Goldisc and Stardust also issued the song.

As the writer of *Three Stars,* Dee collected royalties for all versions of his song. Elvis Presley Music purchased American Music, which originally owned publishing rights to *Three Stars* and *Blue Christmas*, because Elvis wanted to own the rights to the latter after it became a hit for him.

9

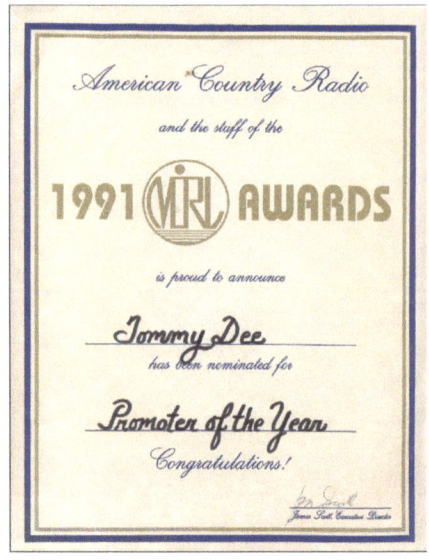

American Country Radio
Award Nomination

Tommy Dee, c. 1996

Tribute songs to Holly, the Bopper, and Valens continue to come out and these are some of the better known songs. Jackie DeShannon (as Jackie Dee) recorded *Buddy* in 1958 while the singer was still alive. Although he recorded the song before Tommy Dee, Eddie Cochran's rendition was not issued until 1966 in the United Kingdom and in 1971 in the United States, when the album *Eddie Cochran* appeared. Hershel Almond offered his own tribute in *The Great Tragedy,* as did Benny Barnes with *Gold Records in the Snow*. Ray Campi's *Ballad of Donna and Peggy Sue* backed with *The Man I Met (Tribute to the Big Bopper)* was issued around March 1959. Ruby

Wright's cover version of *Three Stars* came out as the original was climbing up the charts. In 1959, Donna Dameron had *Bopper 486609,* while the Kittens recorded *A Letter to Donna.*

British singer Mike Berry with the Outlaws had a number 24 hit in the United Kingdom with *A Tribute to Buddy Holly* in 1961, which was also recorded two years later by Chad Allen with the Reflections. Former Crickets' member Waylon Jennings recorded *Stars in Heaven* in 1963, later re-titled *The Stage* and *Old Friend* in 1976. Don McLean gave us *American Pie,* which was the most successful tribute of all. *American Pie* was originally issued on an album at the end of 1971. When issued as a single 45 RPM record in 1972, it became the number 3 record of the year on *Billboard* and the number 1 record of the year on *Cash Box*. Two feature films, *The Buddy Holly Story* and *La Bamba* have also helped immortalize the singers.

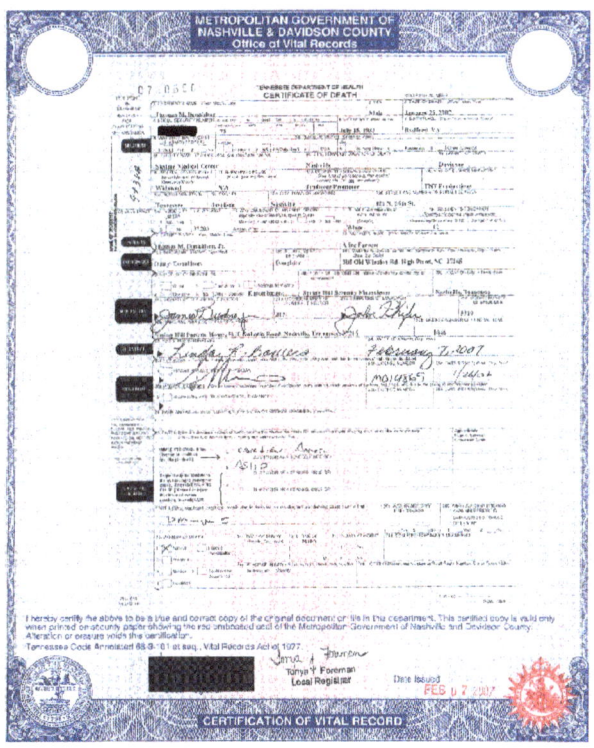

Thomas Donaldson died on January 26, 2007 in Nashville, Tennessee. He was buried with full military honors at the Spring Hill Funeral Home and Cemetery in Nashville.

DISCOGRAPHY

All U.S. issues except as noted

Artist/Song Titles/Release Date/Label & Number

Tommy Dee with Carol Kay and the Teen-Aires
Three Stars/I'll Never Change (Carol Kay and the Teen-Aires only)
2/11/59   Crest 1057   (mono and stereo versions available of above)

Tommy Dee with Teen Tones (reissue)
Three Stars/I'll Never Change (Carol Kay and the Teen Tones only)
Date?   Crest 1057

Tommy Dee with Carol Kay and the Teen-Aires (Canadian pressing)
Three Stars/I'll Never Change (Carol Kay and the Teen-Aires only)
1959   Reo 8354X

Tommy Dee with Carol Kay and the Teen-Aires (Australian pressing)
Three Stars/I'll Never Change (Carol Kay and the Teen-Aires only)
1959   Columbia 45 DO4078

Tommy Dee (Carol Kay and the Teen-Aires are not credited on the labels)
Three Stars/(the other side is *Buzz-Buzz-Buzz* by the Hollywood Flames)
(Canadian pressing)
Date?   Stardust 036

Three Stars/(the other side is *Sandy* by Larry Hall)
Date?   Goldisc G3130

Tommy Dee with Carol Kay and the Teen-Aires
The Chair/Hello, Lonesome
1959   Crest 1061

Tommy Dee with Carol Kay and the Teen-Aires
The Chair/Hello, Lonesome (Canadian pressing)
1959   Reo 8388X

Tommy Dee and Carol Kay
Merry Christmas, Mary/Angel of Love
1959   Crest 1067

Tommy Dee
There's a Star Spangled Banner Waving Somewhere/Hobo and the Puppy
1960   Challenge 59083
Ballad of A Drag Race/The Story of Susie
1960   Challenge 59087
Loving You (On Somebody Else's Time)/Halfway To Hell
1961   Pike 5906
A Little Dog Cried/Look Homeward, Dear Angel
1961   Pike 5909
Look Homeward Dear Angel/Missing On a Mountain
1963   Pike 5917
Look Homeward Dead Angel/Missing On a Mountain
1963   Pike 5917
Look Homeward Dead Angel/Missing On A Mountain (Canadian pressing)
1963   London 17293
Open Letter/She Called Me Baby, Baby All Night Long
1963   Pike
Sheep (recorded for Pike Records
c. 1963, (unissued as a single at the time but released on a White Label Records
LP #8888, a Dutch company, in 1985)
Missing While Surfing/ Goodbye High School
1966   Sims 260
How's Your Mama 'Em/ Goodbye High School
1966   Sims 308

Tommy Dee with Bonita Stevens
The In-Between Train/?
1966?   Label/#?

Tommy Dee
Open Letter/She Called Me Baby, Baby All Night Long
1967?   Little Darlin' #?

School for Boys/Roger, Ed and Gus (America's Astronaut Heroes)
1967   Starday 802

Welfare Cadillac/Puppy and the Hobo
1970   K-Ark 995
Coal Black Coal/Little Lady Coal Miner
Date? Coal Mountain 1017
Baby Rights/?
1993   Label?

This discography is incomplete. Please contact the publisher if you have additions and/or corrections. Thank you.

Tommy Dee and the Mellotones, who recorded the instrumental *Dragonfly* in 1959 on the Lifetime label, are unrelated to this artist. The Tommy Dee of D.O.A. (Dead On Arrival) is also a different artist. *The Idolmaker*, a 1980 film that has a certain similarity to the lives of Fabian and Frankie Avalon, features an actor by the name of Tommy Dee but this is not a reference to the Tommy Dee who is the subject here.

According to the BMI, Inc. files Tommy Dee wrote the following songs

- Angel of Love
- Baby Rights
- Ballad of Black and White
- Bed Side Manner
- Bingo
- Body Language
- Building Bridges
- Cheap Bad Wine
- Cincinnati
- Danny White
- Dig Down Brother
- Eat a Toyota
- Goodbye High School, Hello Vietnam
- Halfway to Hall
- Hang Tuff
- Heading for the River
- Hello Lonesome
- Hey, You're Hurting Me
- Honey Babe
- Honky Tonks and Swinging Doors
- How's You Momma 'Em
- I Did My Duty
- I Lost My Heart In Your Arms Love
- I'm a Bad Bad Girl
- I'm Leaving the Leaving Up to You
- I'm Only Seventeen
- I Never Met a Cowboy I Didn't Like
- I Spent the Nite in the Country
- I Wanna Make Love to You
- If I Follow You Home
- If My Eyes Could Talk
- It's Good To Be Here
- Letting All Her Memories Go
- Like an Oklahoma Morning
- Loving You
- Make Me Your Believer
- Memphis Shroud
- Midnight Rock
- Momma Hid the Bottle
- Babies Stop Your Crying
- Ballad of a Drag Race
- Ballad of O.J. Simpson
- Big Women
- Bingo's Bongo Bingo Party
- Bring Me In Out of the Rain
- Bunny Rabbit
- Child of the World
- Daniel Boone
- Dejesus Gladyces
- Don't Make a Fool Out of Me
- Give Me Something Called Love
- Grab a Hold of the Lord
- Halfway to Hell
- Hanging Heavy On My Mind
- Heart, Body and Soul
- Here's Looking at You Kid
- Hobo and the Puppy
- Honky Tonk House
- How I Love Big Women
- I'd Do Anything For You Baby
- I Got a Lot On My Conscience
- I Love a Boy
- I'm a Brave Little Soldier
- I'm On Your Side
- I'm So Afraid
- I Only Want Your Body
- I've Already Loved You In My Heart
- I Want to Talk to You
- If I Only Have One Life to Live
- It Must Be Love
- Left Over Loving
- Like a Yo Yo Baby
- Look Homeward Dear Angel
- Make Me An Offer I Can't Refuse
- Married Woman Eyes
- Merry Christmas Mary
- Missing on a Mountain
- Mommy's Japanese

Mr. Stubby
My Baby's Back Home
My Name is Tennie
Night Surfin'
Nite Surfin'
Nobody Said It Was Gonna Be Easy
Nobody Somebody
One More Night of Heaven
Onion Man
Open Letter
Our Love is a Phantom
Puppy and the Bear
Roger, Ed and Gus (America's Astronaut Heroes)
Ruby's Answer
S.O.S.
S.O.S. (Same Old Stuff)
School for Fools
Shadow of the Cross
Shadows of Shame
She Forgot to Take Me
She Loved the Hell Right Out of Me
Silly Sue Ann
Singer
Take a Walk Thru the Pain
Taming My Mind
This Old Feeling
Three Stars
Time
Today I Found a Letter
Truck Driver's Last Will and Testament
Twin Pipes
Under the Moon
Until I Can Let Go of the Bottom
Waiting For a Letter From Mama
Wanted A Live in Lover
What's the Matter Mama
Who's That Knocking
Why Can't You Love Me Like Before
Wrap Your Love Around My Heart
Your Place or Mine

ClockTower Publications

Part of a Sound Company founded in 1973

203 Skyland Drive, Suite C
Staunton, Virginia 24401
www.clocktowerpublications.com
trgww@ntelos.net

Publications

A Discography of Rhythm & Blues and Rock & Roll circa 1946-1964 (out-of-print)

A Discography of Rhythm & Blues and Rock & Roll circa 1946-1964: Supplement (out-of-print)

Staunton, Virginia: Vignettes from the Shenandoah Valley's Queen City Volume I

Staunton, Virginia: Vignettes from the Shenandoah Valley's Queen City Volume II

THEATRICS: A Mystery Set In Staunton, Virginia

Staunton Treasures – Past & Present: Connect-The-Dots

Augusta County, Staunton, & Waynesboro Find-A-Word Puzzles

Houses of Worship Augusta County, Staunton, & Waynesboro Find-A-Word Puzzles

The Case of The Missing Menorah (a Sunday School play)

For information about any of the above titles contact the publisher

TRG WorldWide Divisions

CTP MARKETING & LITERARY SERVICES ™

CTP Marketing & Literary Services provides a variety of services to help authors bring their works to market.

The Record Groove ™

The Record Groove markets phonograph records, music CDs, vintage pre-recorded audio-cassettes, music literature and sheet music, rock star pins, and Statler Brothers' memorabilia.

ClockTower Publications ™

ClockTower Publications publishes books of music and local Augusta County interest, and also markets new and used collectable books.

Rockin' All Nite Long ™

Rockin' All Nite Long provides Disc Jockey services for special events including weddings & engagements, birthday parties, family and school reunions, anniversaries, graduations, holidays, retirements, retreats, company functions, community events, fund raisers, and other special occasions.

www.ingramcontent.com/pod-product-compliance
Lightning Source LLC
Chambersburg PA
CBHW042026150426
43198CB00002B/82